BIG MAMA
The World is a Playground Enjoy it!

GWENDOLYN JEVITA CHEATHAM, Ph.D.

Outskirts Press, Inc.
Denver, Colorado

Also by Gwendolyn Jevita Cheatham, Ph.D.
Give Your Teacher This Note: Parents Say the Funniest Things

(Available at all major bookstores and Amazon.com)

The opinions expressed in this manuscript are solely the opinions of the author and do not represent the opinions or thoughts of the publisher. The author has represented and warranted full ownership and/or legal right to publish all the materials in this book.

Big Mama
The World is a Playground--Enjoy it!
All Rights Reserved.
Copyright © 2011 Gwendolyn Jevita Cheatham, Ph.D.
v6.0

Cover Photo © 2011 JupiterImages Corporation. All rights reserved - used with permission.

Photographs on the cover, and throughout this book, are indicative of places that Dr. Gwendolyn Jevita Cheatham has visited during her career as an educator.

This book may not be reproduced, transmitted, or stored in whole or in part by any means, including graphic, electronic, or mechanical without the express written consent of the publisher except in the case of brief quotations embodied in critical articles and reviews.

Outskirts Press, Inc.
http://www.outskirtspress.com

ISBN: 978-1-4327-1192-4

Outskirts Press and the "OP" logo are trademarks belonging to Outskirts Press, Inc.

PRINTED IN THE UNITED STATES OF AMERICA

"Write the things which thou hast seen, and the things which are, and the things which shall be hereafter."

...Revelation 1:19

Dedication

With love and affection, I dedicate this book to my seven sisters, and my brother: Bertha, Alvertiss, Barbara, Beverly, Laverne, Yvonne, Gennie Ruth, and Roy.

Big Mama

I also dedicate this book to all "Big Mamas."

A "Big Mama" can be:
A mother
A stepmother
A mother-in-law
A grandmother
A nana
A guardian
A sister
An aunt
A cousin
A friend
A teacher
A minister
A mentor
A nanny
A neighbor
or
anyone who has touched a person's life in a loving, caring, and meaningful way.

Contents

Preface 1
Quotes to Live By 6
Reflections on Life 45
Poetic Images 65
Big Mama has Something Else to Tell You 122
Acknowledgements 161
About the Photographs 163
Index of Titles 165
About the Author 175

Preface

This book is a compilation of original quotes, reflections, and poetry. I use the term, "Big Mama," to represent one who has touched a person's life in a loving, caring, and meaningful way.

I have always seen the world as a very fascinating and enigmatic playground. When I am in a dilemma, or wish to address an issue, I turn to my love for writing. The comfort I find in writing has sustained me throughout my life.

An important facet of my approach to life comes from women who surrounded me during my formative years, including my mother, sisters, aunts, grandparents, cousins, clergy, teachers, close neighbors, and friends of the family. I, affectionately, refer to these women as *Big Mama*.

If "Big Mama" said it,
then, it's definitely true.
(Well, maybe.)

The world is a playground.
Enjoy it !

Boating is an awesome adventure!

Quotes to Live By

Truthfulness

It is better to be truthful,
and reveal your little
short story, than to
turn a lie into
a novel.

Be Kind

Be kind to everyone.
You never know what
burdens they are
carrying.

Writing

Writing is the purest
expression of freedom.

Poet

Ordinary writers speak
from the heart. Poets speak
from the soul. When the heart
and soul unite, a unique and
magnificent masterpiece
is born.

Journey

Life is a journey encompassing
a vast number of experiences.
These experiences create
a beautiful poem.

Coward

There is a difference between being
cautious, prudent, and discreet and
being an outright unequivocal,
unmitigated coward.

Friendship

A person is either your friend,
or the person is not. There is
no middle ground
in friendship.

Admiring and Possessing

One can admire something
beautiful without wishing
to covet, or possess it.

Jokes

It's okay to laugh
at a joke; however,
don't become
the joke.

Your Children

Never give up on your
precious children.

Taste of Freedom

Once a person gets a taste
of freedom, that person
is never the same.

Appreciation

Love is shown in many ways.
There is no reason to pout
if you do not hear the words,
"I love you." everyday.

Suntan

Single men's fingers
suntan all over.

Getting to Know a Man

If you want to know a man's
character, his heart, and
his spirit, pay close attention to
how he treats the women
in his family.

Misfortunes

Misfortunes are incidents
that happen to you beyond
your control. They do not
define who you are.

Women's Strength

A woman's strength is her
inner beauty, her dignity, her
sweetness, and her grace.

Curfews

If you allow your child
to ignore your curfews,
eventually, your child
will ignore you.

Showing Off

Learn from flowers. Notice how they always know when it's time to bloom. They never rush to show off their colors.

Saying and Doing

What little you are doing is so loud that I cannot hear what you are saying.

Walking

Don't ask how long it will take to walk a mile. Ask how long it will take to walk a few yards at a time.

Children are Different

Children are different. Some children are shy. Others are outgoing. Let them be themselves. Don't push them to be who they were not meant to be.

Time

One of the greatest mistakes people can make is to waste their time. It is sacred, and can never be recovered.

Loving

You cannot persuade a person to love you. That is something the person must do on their own.

Learning

If you want to learn a skill, practice it. The more you practice, the sooner the skill will be mastered. There is no shortcut.

Baking Cookies

No matter how successful a woman is, there's always the lady inside her who would much rather be at home baking cookies.

QUOTES TO LIVE BY

Schools
Schools should be a visual and dynamic microcosm of the community they serve.

Prom night should be safe.

I Believe

Everyone is a child of God.
There is dignity in all persons.
Circumstances mold character.
Life is meant to be
lived, joyfully.

Your Dreams

If you don't follow your dreams,
you'll never know how awesome
you might have become.

DNA and LOVE

Father is spelled: D-N-A.
Dad is spelled: L-O-V-E.

Crisis

People who will not help
their friends, when they are
confronted with a crisis,
should not come around
later to ask them how
things turned out.

Sap
Sometimes, the person who looks like a sap is really the one who closes the gap, and walks away with the prize.

Heartbreak
Only the people you love can break your heart.

Apples
Some apples don't just fall "a little far from the tree." They never leave it.

Years and Days
The years teach us so much that the days will soon forget.

Truth
Sometimes, it isn't easy to hear the truth. Think before you ask the question.

Ladies and Gents

There is no excuse for abuse!
There is no excuse for abuse!!
There is no excuse for abuse!!!
Is that loud enough?

Self Esteem and Ego

Self-esteem is not innate. It is developed as one encounters life's challenges. The ego, when inflated, signifies self-centeredness and conceit. It is not the same as self-esteem.

Your Faults

Avoid people who highlight your faults, your faux pas, and your frailties and never mention your enormous strengths.

Stick in the Mud

A stick in the mud will always remain only a stick in the mud. It will never transform itself into a gentleman's fine walking cane.

Becoming A Parent

At what point in your life did you say, "Oh, my goodness! I have now become my mother, my father?"

Be Yourself

Be yourself, or frustrate yourself trying to be someone else.

Know It All

A person who thinks they know everything has learned nothing from life.

Talking Out Loud

If you can't tell someone something to their face, don't say it behind their back. Only cowards and gossips put others down while trying to uplift themselves.

Talking to Children

The moment you stop talking
to your children is the exact
moment they begin to talk
to someone else.

I'm Sorry

Don't apologize for anything
that was not your fault.

Good Old Common Sense

Good old common sense
supersedes all, so-called,
intelligence, wisdom,
and sagacity.

Stars

Stars will twinkle in the sky,
whether you pay attention
to them, or not. It is the same
way with ambitious people.
Nothing holds them back.
They are driven to succeed
and achieve excellence.

Friends

One good friend is better than several dubious and disloyal acquaintances.

Remedy

There is a remedy for ignorance; however, stupidity can be a terminal illness that goes straight to the marrow of the bones.

Open Mind

Before dismissing everything that wise, elderly persons say as foolishness, listen to them. Keep an open mind. They have a life time of experience.

Friendships

Friendships that destroy, deface, or subvert your smile should be examined for their authenticity.

Be Quiet
Sometimes, you listen.
Sometimes, you speak.
Listen or speak, not both.

Acceptance
Accept people for who
they are, not for what you
want to fashion them
into becoming.

Nations
Nations should be very
careful how they treat their
children. Someday, these
children will become
adults, and they
will remember.

Baggage
If a person comes to you
with a lot of baggage, ask them
to wait for the next train.

Respect Children

Respect children for their uniqueness. They are all different and beautiful in their own way.

Snakes

Snakes bite, even when they have been fed. Some humans have the same qualities as snakes.

Icy Weather

You seldom see squirrels searching for food when there is ice on the ground. They work while the sun is shining.

Past • Present • Future

Don't live in the past.
Live in the present.
Plan for the future.
Be happy.
Live now!

Birds Share

Watch the birds. Notice how they will take only one worm. They don't grab all of them for themselves.

River of Love

There is a river called—LOVE. Its desire is to flow through the heart of everyone. Pause and savor its richness.

Nasty Words

If I say something nasty about someone, should those words make me feel cleaner?

Criticism

Don't criticize your spouse, if you are still living in the house.

Little Voice

A little voice in your head says, "Don't do this." Listen to that little voice.

Purchasing a Car

You will not improve your driving habits by purchasing a new car. It's the same in life. You've got to get behind the wheel.

Things You Don't Need to Teach

There are some things you don't need to teach:
A baby how to cry.
A bird how to fly.
A deacon how to have a fish fry.

Attitude

Some people have every reason in the world to have a bad attitude, to be angry, sad, aloof, and reclusive; however, they have chosen to be optimistic, to have a positive attitude, and to possess a sweet spirit.

Creativity

A person's most important asset is their ability to be very imaginative and creative. This is the birth of progress.

Owing

You owe nothing to anyone, unless something was promised to them.

Pressure

Are you really under a lot of pressure, or are you saying, Yes. too many times, to friends and family?

Writing and Knowing

If you can't write it, you don't really know it.

Mankind

All human beings are the sum of everyone and everything that has ever touched their life.

Spending Time

Unless quality time is spent with a person, you don't really know them.

Burdens

When our burdens become too much to bear, it seems that some divine force takes over and carries them for us.

Forgiveness

Forgive yourself for the silly things you did during your youth. You were just a child, trying to find your way.

Wars

If men were not able to wage war and destroy one another, what new game would these men invent?

Losing

You lost. So what! At least, you had the courage to get in the game.

Cougars

Advice to Lady Cougars While on a date with your younger man, don't ask the waiter for the senior discount.

Dreams

If you have a dream, go after it with all your might. If it turns into a nightmare, get over it! Pursue another dream. Don't ever give up!

Best Friend

A girl's *first* best friend should be her mother, or her guardian.

Pay the Price

The price of freedom; the price of a good education; the price of keeping your dignity; and the price of valor is great. Will you pay the price?

✧✧✧

World's Problems

Don't try to solve the world's problems. If you solve your own, the world will take care of itself.

✧✧✧

Listen and Learn

There are many things that you already know. *Listen* and learn even more.

✧✧✧

Feelings

If a person doesn't like you, it doesn't matter how much you do for them. They will still feel disdain towards you.

✧✧✧

Fortune Cookie

You are responsible for your own life. You have the power to determine what your future will portray. Your life is not what you find in a fortune cookie.

Deck of Cards

Life deals you a hand, and you should play it as best you can.

Animals

Learn from the animals. They don't judge people for their exterior beauty. They like people for what they sense is coming from the heart.

Confident People

Confident people know exactly who they are. They are courageous and proud. You accept them, or they move on.

Rainbow

The world is made of a beautiful rainbow of many different people, speaking to one another in various languages. These people create a majestic, radiant, enchanting, and glorious symphony.

Understanding

When you want to understand something, you must take it apart, examine it, study it, and put it back together again.

Challenges

Why be afraid of challenges? They strengthen one's spirit.

Courage

All humans seek courage. It comes from deep within one's soul, and rises through the mind into the spirit.

Respect

Sometimes, it's necessary
to tell a person not to confuse
you with someone for whom
they have very little regard,
or no respect at all.

Jumping Off the Cliff

You can admire the valley,
without jumping off the cliff.

Weeds

All pretty flower beds get ugly
weeds--from time to time.

Something for Nothing

If you think you got something
for nothing, you probably did;
however, you can't figure out
what the something is
that you got.

Best Friends

Most people look a lot
like their best friend.

Re-invent Yourself

Re-invent yourself everyday by improving on your yesterdays, and your tomorrows.

Honesty and Integrity

Honesty and integrity are identical twins. When you see one, you will also see the other one.

Respect at Home

Respect in the privacy of your own home is as important as respect in public places.

Character

Your reputation is what people see you do. Your character is who you really are. Who are you, really? Balance your reputation with your character.

Bully

A bully hopes the image
in front of him will
go away before
he gets to it.

Flutes

At times, you can't hear the
sound of the lovely flutes for the
loud beating of the drums.

Seeing

You didn't see it.
You can't describe it.
Don't discuss it.

Accumulating Stuff

People spend the first half of
their life accumulating stuff,
and the last half of their
life getting rid of it.

Licking Your Wounds

It's natural to lick your wounds
after being hurt; however,
don't lick them until the flesh
begins to fall off.

Good Morning

When a person says, "Good morning." they are not asking for the whole story.

~~~

Kissing Frogs

You should *not* kiss a lot of frogs before you find your *Prince*.

~~~

Wise Man

What a wise man does not understand, he studies; what he learns, he shares with those who have no access to pedagogy.

~~~

Family

No one can choose the family into which they are born. Be content with who you are.

~~~

Love
Love needs space to evolve,
maturate, and blossom.

Your Joy
No one stole your joy.
It was your own doing.
You wrapped it up in a
pretty package and
gave it away.

Sheep
A sheep is not the only animal
that will follow another animal
to the chopping block.

Power
Most women are not aware
of the power they possess.

Take Over
If your group is divided,
anyone can take over and
exploit it. The same is
true for families.

Opinion

A person's opinion should always be respected in their own home.

Mama's Boy

Don't dismiss every *mama's boy* as a perpetual mama's boy. By doing so, you might, possibly, overlook a very stable, sensitive, and responsible man. Listen to your mind *and* your heart.

Trump Card

In life, you don't play your trump card until you need it.

Mile in Someone's Shoes

Walk a mile in someone else's shoes. From that day forward, you might want to go barefoot.

Genius

If both parents have an average IQ, they should not expect to give birth to a genius.

Good Man

Before you let that good man go, you might want to take a walk around the marketplace and check out the other goods.

Lending Money

If you lend money to a friend or a family member, you should consider it a gift. It is quite likely that you will never see it again.

Tamed Horses

One tamed horse is worth five undomesticated, rampageous, wild ones. Numbers do not always define success.

Possessing and Owning

It is not what you possess,
but what you own
that counts.

Cognizant

Be cognizant of the forces in
your life that could turn
around and bite you.

Alarm Clocks

Isn't it intriguing how
mothers don't need
an alarm clock to know
when it's time to get up
in the morning?

Common Sense

Know this: Common sense
does not always come with a
college education. Some
people just happen to know
when certain things do not
make any sense.

Documentation

Document all the documentation.
Then, make copies of the documents
that you documented. Finally,
document the fact that you filed
the documents away, and that
everything was documented.

Whisper

A whisper can
be louder than
a shout.

Mean People

Nice people fall asleep easily.
Mean people lie awake,
thinking of more mean
things to do.

Fixing People

Before you attempt to *fix*
others, make sure you
have *fixed* yourself.

Solomon

Solomon's creed: If you have wisdom and knowledge, then riches will come.

Life

Life is crystal clear. People muddy it up by trying to change it to look like something it is not.

People

People are not always what they appear to be. It takes time to become well acquainted with another person.

Reflection

When you look in the mirror do you like the reflection, or are you looking for a better person?

Worthwhile

Do something worthwhile and meaningful each and every day.

Work

Everyone *should* know who did the hard work. This exposes free-loaders at the work place.

Keys

A good man's keys will always open his own front door.

Being Right

It's better to be right and alone, than to be wrong in a crowd.

Broken Mirrors

Broken mirrors only bring bad luck when you step on them and cut your foot.

Traps

Be careful where you
set your traps. One day,
you might decide to
go for a walk and, unwarily,
get your own feet caught
in the snare.

Liars and Thieves

Liars and thieves have
the same ugly face.

House and Home

It takes many years
to make a house
a true home.

Key to Success

Get up!
Get dressed!
Go to work!
Make a dollar!
Save a quarter!
This is the key
to success.

Words
Words are powerful. Be certain that every word you utter has meaning.

Arrogance
Arrogance is a combination of insecurities within oneself, and an inflated ego.

Who are You?
You are not always who people think you are. You are who you know in your heart that you are.

Absolutely Sure
If you are absolutely sure you are right, what does it matter what others say about you?

Happiness
Ultimately, we are all responsible for our own happiness.

Meet the Date

It's a good idea to meet
your child's mate before
they leave for the date.

Mind Your Business

Mind your own business.
Watch the time fly by.
There's no time remaining
to mind anyone else's.

Living Right

The more you live right,
the fewer times you
will need to say,
"I was wrong."
"Forgive me."
"I'm sorry."

Little Bit of something

A little bit of something
is worth more than
a whole barrel
of nothing.

◄ BIG MAMA

Space to Grow
If you love someone,
give them space to think,
to meditate, and
to grow.

Sacre Coeur Cathedral (Paris, France at Montmartre)

Reflections on Life

The Thinker, by Auguste Rodin. (Rodin Gardens in Paris, France)

Beautiful Things

Beautiful things remind us
of the people we love.

Prophet

During famine and war, a Prophet
is sent to his people. He comes
from afar, mixed with the
blood of many peoples. He
is from everywhere, and
from out of nowhere.
He emerges to save
his people from their
unfortunate fate.

Affirmative Action
(According to My Mother)

My mother said, "Your three
older sisters and your brother
went to college. You are
going to college, too."
I said, "Yes, ma'am."
My mother said it!
I affirmed it!
The conversation was *over!*
That was my mother's
interpretation of
Affirmative Action.

Prayer

I like to pray early in the morning,
when God is probably
less busy.

Your Heart

Guard your heart. Keep
it safe from harm. Once
it is broken, it's hard to
put it back together.

Me • Myself • I

Sometimes, it's necessary
to sit and talk with me, in
order to get myself and I
back on track.

Child Abuse

Children never fully recover from abuse.
Parents who abuse their children
never get to know what beautiful,
awesome, and brilliant people
they brought into
the world.

Projects

I enjoy the feeling I have when I have given my all to a particular project, then realize its successful completion.

❧❧❧

Rocking the Boat

There are some people who will never *rock* the boat. They will not *steer* the boat. They will not *dock* the boat. They will not *clean* the boat. However, when the boat goes off course, they are the first to say, "You don't know anything about boats."

❧❧❧

Betrayal

When a friend betrays you, it is a milestone in your life. You are never the same. It changes your entire world, forever!

❧❧❧

MUSIC

Slow down and listen to the music.
It has a soothing effect on the spirit.
All music comes from one individual
who searches deep into the soul
for perfection. When the score is
composed, this person looks upward
towards heaven and gives
thanks for the melody.

Five Wars

I was five at the start of the Korean War.
I lived through the Vietnam War.
I survived the Desert Storm War.
I am witnessing the perils of the Iraq War,
and the Afghanistan War.
After living through all these wars,
I will let no one place limitations
on me, or tell me what I am
not able to accomplish.

Time for a Friend

With all the chaos we face
everyday, why not take some
time for a family member, or a
very loyal and dear friend?

REFLECTIONS ON LIFE

Why African American Women Wear Hats

It occurred to me that, perhaps,
African American women
wear hats because these hats
are reminiscent of our
African ancestry.

How sassy and beautiful
those women must have been,
strutting around the market place
with children resting on their
backs and their clay pottery,
teeming with vegetables,
bouncing rhythmically,
on top of their heads.

African woman with pottery and kente cloth dress.

Defining Yourself

Refuse to be defined by who others say you are. Don't be afraid. Step out into the waters of life. Get wet. Dry off. Then, dive into the deep end.

Great Books

Great books are read for their intrigue, depth, and intensity. They make us think, envision, and change magnanimously.

Grieving

When one grieves too long, the souls of loved ones cannot rest in peace. Know when it's time to live again.

Squirrels

Take note of squirrels. They don't make noise as they work. They focus.

Your Life

Examine your life. If there is anything holding you back, let it go. Move on.

Some People are Crazy

You are introduced to someone. Right away, there is the distinct impression that the person is crazy. Don't try to dress it up by saying that they are strange, bizarre, eccentric, or even a little bit different. They are crazy. C—R—A—Z—Y!

Beware

Beware of people who greet you with: "I need." "Can you?" "May I borrow?" "Will you do this for me?" "I need your help real bad." They are users. Don't be a cash-cow, or a sap.

Pay Back

A daughter, or a son, who phones their mother complaining about the children should not be surprised when the mother replies to them, "Pay back is hell, isn't it?"

HAITI

As I pray, I cry for our brothers and sisters in Haiti who stand in line for a can of oil and a small sack of rice. Now, there is a greater challenge: overcoming the devastation of the earthquakes. Keep the faith, friends.

Children Grow Up

A child leaves home to see the world. When the child returns, this child is an adult. At some point, you will need to let your child grow up.

Flowers

Flowers are a gift from God.
They should not be taken for
granted. Notice the wonder of
the colors, and the variety
of fragrances. Be grateful
for them. They are
God's miracles!

Human Heart

The capacity of the human
heart for evil, astounds me.

Gifted

Anyone can dust a Rembrandt;
however, it takes a gifted individual
to create a reverent masterpiece.

True Friends

True friends don't wait until a
crisis is over before
they comfort you.
They are there for you
every step of the way.

Excellence

Everyone can achieve excellence. When a person has given their all to a worthwhile task, they have done this with excellence. Be courageous in your pursuit of excellence.

Guardian Angels

Guardian angels are always with us. They watch over us and surround us with their love and care.

God Created Woman

When God created woman, He took the rib from the man's side; not from the front of the man's body, and not from the back of the man's body. A woman is a man's partner. She walks proudly with the man, side by side.

Reading

If you *can* read, but you *don't* read, look in the mirror and admit that you are *illiterate*.

Psychiatrist or Lawyer

So, he said, "You are one *crazy* lady, and you need a psychiatrist." You don't need a psychiatrist. You need a lawyer!

Feeling Down

When I feel down, I shop for things that lift me up. When I feel better, I return these things to the store.

It is Your Life

Be careful who you allow to step into your life and take a seat. It is your life. It does not belong to just anyone who decides to take it over.

Guilt

Why do women feel guilty when they are not working, or doing something for someone other than themselves? Men are not that way. They seldom feel guilty about anything.

Letters and Emails

In lieu of sending an email to a friend today, why not write them a personal letter?

Time for Yourself

Set aside some time during the work day for yourself. Reflect. Read. Write. Pray. Give thanks.

Your Name

There is nothing more important than your name. Your name is the essence of who you are. It is the root of your being. Respect for your name

tells everyone you meet
that you are proud to be
called by your name.

If your name is tainted,
you have lost a part of your
innate spirit. Generations
to come will honor you,
or not, by your name.

Be cognizant of what
you do, where you go,
what you say, and how
you choose to behave.
You are representing yourself
as well as those who
came before you.

Your ancestors were proud,
determined, and dignified.
Their toils, sweat, and sacrifices
helped to establish the family's
name. People will watch you.
They will scrutinize you.
They will criticize you.
Then, they will call
your name.

Architecture

Beautiful architecture is seductive. It resembles exhilarating, sensuous, frozen music.

Living Life

Don't live your life sitting on the sidelines, wondering what's going on. Get up! Join in the fun!

Misbehaving

Some parents ask, "Are those my children, acting like they have no home training?" "Yes. They are yours."

Milestones

In everyone's life, there are milestones. Approach each milestone as a challenge. Stick to your goals. Accept the gift that God had prepared for you. Some gifts are positive, and

some are negative. Be
courageous. Avoid being
pessimistic.

Hug yourself every morning
and say, "This is the day that
the Lord Almighty has made. I
will rejoice and be glad in it.
No matter what happens,
I will enjoy this day.
Although there are many
things on my To Do List, I
am going to do them
with efficiency, joy,
and love."

She Ain't Mean

An old lady sat on her porch.
The rumor among the neighborhood
children was, *The old lady who
stared at them from her rickety,
dilapidated front porch was
very mean and scary.*

The children always ran
swiftly by her house. They
stopped waving at her because

she never waved back at them. Her blank stare frightened them. From the street, they could not see her bruised, twisted hands and the bend in her back.

A new boy moved into the neighborhood. He passed by the old lady's house and waved at her. Feeling somewhat tired from his long walk from school, he asked the old lady if he could sit on her porch for a while. She nodded.

The old lady began to talk. She told the new boy the story of her life. The next day, the new boy told the other children the old lady's life story. They insisted that she was still only a mean old lady. The new boy replied, "She ain't mean. She's tired. That's all."

The author visits Little Rock Central High School where her aunt, Daisy Bates, mentored The Little Rock Nine.

L'Ombre (The Shadow) *by Auguste Rodin*

A gift from France to the Atlanta Memorial Museum, after a fatal plane crash at Orly Airport in Paris. One hundred and six Atlanta artists perished there.

Poetic Images

Birds are on Fire
[September 11, 2001]

The ringing phones filled the air.
Loved ones were waiting there to
say goodbye: *Mom, dad, my love,
I will not make it home today,
not to the one you made for me,
but to one more beautiful
than words can say.*

Those who were blessed, survived.
Others helped to save lives.
On the streets, some looked
on in disbelief, while
others sadly expressed
their profound grief.
It was such a terrifying day,
as hundreds of people ran away.
Glass and bricks flew after them
through the dark and dusty film.
A river of tears were soothed as a
priest came near and moved among
the crowd offering prayers, telling
everyone how much he cared.
Before noon of that day,
he was also taken away.

This holy man did not die alone.
He joined the others on the way
to their heavenly home.

Children looked up at the sky
with their beautiful, innocent,
tear-filled eyes—and cried:
*"Teacher, look! The birds
are on fire! The birds are
on fire!"* The teacher knew
that the birds were not
on fire. It was someone's
sister, brother, husband,
or wife fleeing the
misery and the
strife on...
...September 11,
2001.

Hero Has Died

The bagpipes blast
their sweetest sounds,
and the crowds
gather swiftly around.
A hero has died.
The tears flow
beneath their eyes.

This war is despised.
A hero has died.

Bagpipers play in rain,
sunshine, and snow—
their loyalty to show for
the hero who has died.
It's someone's sister,
brother, or friend.
The pain of loss begins.
A hero has died.

Bagpipers are our
blessed ones. They march
towards the setting sun
for those whose
hero has died.
Their pipes are filled
with a sad, sad song.
For their loved ones,
they all long. A hero
has died a long
way from home.
It does not matter
about their fame, or
from whence they came.
A hero has died.
The bagpipes ring out

sounds of sorrow,
across the far and
distant waters.

A hero is dying,
somewhere, today.
Over there, they
must not stay.
Bring them home.
Bring them home.

The author visits the Vietnam Memorial in Washington, D. C.

Statue of Liberty

Our Lady stands proudly.
Her light glows in the distance.
She is mighty. She demands respect.
Nations look up to her. Her country
sets their sails towards foreign lands,
laden with arms to spread democracy.
We are the chosen ones. We are the
saviors. We save the destitute, the poor,
and the untutored. They are welcome:
The darker skinned with twisted
braids and velutinous hair; those
who sail on rickety boats; those who
through the thicket and boscages
come, tearing their flesh; and those
speaking in their dialect and patois.
They are all welcome here. Our Lady
greets them with a raised torch in
her hand. She calls her country, the
UNITED STATES OF AMERICA.

War

He went off to war when his
daughter was only five. Her mother
said he would survive. The war
is important she had heard, to
bring peace to the entire world.
The little girl cried many days

before he left. Her mother was
sad. She also wept. He was gone
for a year to this far away place.
When his plane landed
there was a big smile on his
face. The little girl ran to meet
her dad. Her eyes lit up. She
was so glad. He picked her
up in his big, strong arms
and gave her a kiss.
He thought of everything
that he had missed:
Her birthday, her
schooling, her "Good
morning, dad."
All those empty moments
made him feel sad. She
peeped into his ear and
saw grains of sand. There
were also scars on his hand.
She wanted him home, but he
still lacked one more year before
he would be back. Her mother
hugged him, tenderly. She
missed him, too, you see.
"He's serving his country."
she was thinking. He said,
"I love you." Her heart was

sinking. A tear rolled down her
face. "Be strong, my dear.
We'll win this tumultuous race.
We'll be a family again, and
start over from the beginning."
His wife smiled and hugged
his neck. She dreamed of the
day that he'd be back.

Harvard Tale
(Summer, 1994)

When in July the crape myrtles bloom,
and the rain pierces the drought to the root.
All the flowers in Harvard Yard show
their faces to young scholars who pick them
with delight. Lads and their ladies
steal kisses en route to classes where
profs await them with centuries of wisdom,
gathered from those before them. And
specially, from every part of the country
they came to seek the mystique
of aged Harvard.

It happened in that season that we
came, too: seven men and nine ladies
there were—from Connecticut, California,

POETIC IMAGES

Virginia, Vermont, Illinois, New York,
Pennsylvania, New Hampshire,
Hawaii, Maryland, Florida,
New Jersey, and from the state of
Georgia—there were three.

On Harvard's lovely campus, we
found that nine libraries abound.
We read with vigor each day and
night. The verses of Sophocles,
and Oedipus' curses gave us a
fright! Sappho, with odes so
deep that for days on end,
they rocked us to sleep.
We learned that Pindar, the Greatest,
was the real one who had sung of
victories of the old and the
young. Bacchus, the Naughty,
called Dionysus by some, put life into
parties he held at his home. Odysseus,
the Mighty, pretending to be good,
left Troy and sacked a city
as soon as he could.

Plato's shadows put us in the dark,
and Aristotle's *Poetics and Ethics*
left their mark. The Greek alphabet
we learned right away, and started

to translate from the very first day.
Le mot juste we looked for in every
strophe and the lyre became
the musician's trophy.

The Furies and Harpies we learned
to fear, and the magic of Dido
was introduced here.
Aeneas left Carthage fast and far,
but returned to take it in the Third
Punic War. We were entertained
by "Fields of Gold" so sweet,
while at the same time, we
studied the Greeks. On the road
back from Troy, Helen stopped
to shop in lovely Egypt,
so dear. Menelaus shouted:
"We've got to get out of here."
Venus seduces her beloved
with a kiss, but when her lips
were ready for a repay, he winks
at her, and turns his lips away.
Drink from the fountain while
the water flows. A tale we will
tell of Harvard Square: The
hustle, the bustle, flowers
blooming, and majestic statues
in the Yard. Drink from the

esteemed fountain of wisdom;
such sagacity, with which we
could never begin to
measure our own.

Chaucer would say this about
our learned Harvard professor:
He was some fifty years of age,
I guessed. In statue, he was of
moderate length, with wonderful
agility and strength. His spirit
was as fresh as the month of May.
He could sing songs and poems
recite, in many languages.
He was a true scholar.
He taught, eloquently.
He was our friend.
He was our knight.
He was the best.
Professor Nagy.

BIG MAMA

What are You Going to Do With Your Freedom?

What are you going to
do with your freedom,
now that the man
has deemed it so?

What are you going to do
with your freedom?
What are you going to do,
and where will you go?

I heard that there's a boat
that will take me away.
It's much better than this place,
or so they say. When I land on
the other side, I'll be truly free.
My brothers, sisters, wife and
children--I'm hoping to see!

I'm going to build me a castle,
way up high in the sky.
I'm going to plant me some cotton,
and it's going to be all mine.

I'm going to sit and rest my feet.
I'll prop them up on a big high seat.

I'm going to strut right down the street
with my head in the air, and imagine
that I was never back there.

I'm going to raise my hands
to the heavens above, and thank
the Lord for his everlasting love.
I'm going to pack my belongings,
and leave this cursed place.
I'm going to find
my wife and children
and rid myself of
this disgrace.

I'm going to fall on my
bloody knees, and kiss God's
earth. Then, I'll sit and ponder
how to start a new birth.

What are you going to
do with all that
new freedom?

Back to Africa, I'm planning
to go. I've packed my bags.
I'll need to hurry, though.
The old ship won't wait for me.
When I get there, I'll be truly free.

It's my mama and papa
I'm yearning to see.

Since I'm no longer a pitiful
slave, I'm going to search
for who I once was until
I go to my grave.

L'Enfant
(Child)

A child—born in darkness.
Ebony's conception!
Victimized by selfish egos
that aggrandize their own
persuasions, disguised
as those who care for you.

I will teach you the ways of
the masked sage and the erudite,
who prey on feeble, unripe fruit
blossoming slowly— bearing
welts from deprivation.

They stand tall while you
bend beneath onxy'd skies--
supporting centuries of
repetitious, unfulfilled,

lost reveries that will
haunt them, forever.
Beware. They are not who they
purport to be. Behind the mask,
cached away, are found ancient,
frigid statues that expose their
diaphanous chagrin.

Two Soldiers

Her little boy liked to play cops
and robbers, but being a soldier was
his favorite hobby. He went off to
war to serve his nation, and to
make things better for another
generation. He wrote his mother
everyday, and savored the time
he was away. She enjoyed hearing
from her military son, and bragged
to everyone, "He'll be home
when the war is done."
Then, she began to worry
about her beloved one.

The military sent news she'd
learned to dread: *One soldier,
he's missing or wounded--
two, he is dead!* There was

BIG MAMA

a knock at her front door.
An ominous message they bore:
*"We have some bad news for you.
Your son did not make it through."*
She screamed, "No! No!
Not two. Not two."

~~~~

Vietnam Memorial Washington, D. C.

Marquette Park
(Chicago, 1960's)

Freedom fighters,
freedom fighters.
Don't you know they're
waiting for you? Please
don't go to
Marquette Park.

Freedom fighters heard,
but turned their heads.
If I can't be free,
I'd rather be dead in
Marquette Park.

They are all dressed up
in police clothes.
They have guns and dogs
and water hoses.

"We'll throw you in jail."
I heard them say.
Please, stay away
from Marquette Park.
Freedom fighters marched
hundreds strong, but it

wasn't long before they
heard the song:
"Blacks, blacks!
You'd better go home!"
Then, they unleashed
the dogs on them.

Children were screaming.
The asphalt was steaming,
in the heat of the day.
Freedom fighters prayed:
"Lord, Lord come what
may, on the way
to Marquette Park."
An elderly, frail woman
slipped and fell
when she reached
for the child she'd held,
on the hot, wet road
to freedom trail.
Then, the dogs
attacked them.

A black man looked around
and with a frown, he states:
"White folks in Mississippi
need to come to Chicago
to learn how to hate."

Then, the guards opened
the prison gates.

Rocks, sticks, stones, and
bricks--such barbaric weapons
used by hate-filled tribes
cursing the children of the
first earth child.

Freedom! Freedom! Where
do you hide? Will this violence
and hatred ever subside?

The author and a colleague are teachers in the movie, Boy King.

Our Darkest Hour

When we face our darkest hour
and life seems too much to bear,
we remember a life gone swiftly,
though serenely; yet, it still

makes us question God's love
and care. Then, the light shines
through the dark clouds, and
we know God was always there.
Grieve a while, then let go,
gently. Our loved ones'
souls are at *their best* when
we put *our* grieving to rest.
Seize life's moments.
They quickly flee. Savor the
sweet fragrance of every flower
and tree. Much too soon the
night will fall, and our name—
the Lord will also call.

Clean My Garage

I want to clean my garage
before I die. It's on my To Do
List, but I peep in and sigh.
Cleaning a garage is such a chore.
There are boxes and crates galore.
Goodness, gracious!
It's such a bore.

A friend put an old sofa there
before leaving town, and the
piles of garden tools make

me frown. I found a vat that
was used to catch the rain,
and an old red, rusty train.

My car is parked in the driveway
because the garage is a
wreck, I must say.
I get caught in the rain
rushing to my own front door.
I want to pull into the garage
with the things from the store.
My house is as neat as can be,
but the garage makes me
want to scream. If you know
someone who needs work,
I'll hire them quickly
before I go berserk. I want to
clean my garage before I die,
but the thought of it makes
me want to cry.

When they come for me
in those long black cars,
I hope to heck they won't
look in my garage.

Take Me Back to Mother Africa

Take me back to Mother Africa,
where the cool breeze blows my hair.
Take me back to Mother Africa.
My ancestors are waiting
for me there.

Take me back to Mother Africa,
for too long I've missed
the sun that warms the roofs
of the huts, straw-strung.
I miss the children as they
play, and jump, and run,
under the African sun.

Take me back to Mother Africa.
My heart and soul are in that land.
I want to smell the African violets.

I'll touch the warm, powdery
sand in Mother Africa's land.

Take me back to Mother Africa
where my skin glistens from the
morning dew. Take me back to
Mother Africa. For centuries,
its beauty, I never knew.

Listen closely. Can you
hear it? That's Mother Africa's
cry for the children taken from
her bosom, and tossed
overboard to die.

Their blood turned the ocean red.
Beneath the deck, some
lay on their death bed.

Others, snatched from
Mother Africa's hands, now
live in a foreign land.

Catching Up With Myself
[From Parents to Children]
I think it's time to sit and dine.
Perhaps, I'll have a glass of wine.
I'll pick up where the clock
ceased and my tasks increased,
while I lost myself.

Through space and time,
I've missed the years—
and yes, I've shed the tears
'midst all my fears for you,
while I lost touch
with myself.

BIG MAMA

Depressed and stressed
from hearing your woes,
tales of your friends
and your foes—losing
all the while the urge
to listen to myself.

Your lives became a part
of mine. All my dreams were
left behind. I forgot what it
meant to know, how the lilies
and the rosebuds grow,
after the snow.

Taking a break on the Avenue Champs Elysees in Paris, France.

I was too kind to say,
"How did I lose my way,
tending to you day after day?"
The years have passed by,
and I sit here and sign.
At times, I want to cry
while I try to catch up
with myself.

How did I lose myself in you?
My selflessness shined through.

I gave much too little to me.
Now I see who I must be.
Is it too late to recapture the
years I spent tending to my little
dears? I wouldn't trade it for anything.
What happiness they did bring.

Life is great!

◁ BIG MAMA

"If you enter this world knowing you are loved and you leave this world knowing the same, then everything that happens in between can be dealt with."

... Michael Jackson

POETIC IMAGES

Ode to Michael Jackson

BIG MAMA

What impish demon caught you
in its snare, stole your innocence,
and left you there? What
maladies consumed your time?

What evil design led
you down a loathsome path,
and like a rogue, took
away your laugh?

Your eyes teemed with
bitter tears, revealing
all of your fears.
What maniacal thing
made you steal away, and
led you astray?

*They tried, but could not take
your rhythm and your style.
My dear, you only wanted
to rest a while.*

*You chose the earth as your
eternal love, and focused on
the entire world. We watched
in awe at your ability
to transcend into an orbit
we could never reach.*

*You did far more than
you needed to do.
As the years passed,
you grew and grew.*

Fifty years, we were given.
You were so driven.
Through trials and
tribulations, you faced your
frustrations and conquered your
fears. Then, you went quietly
away, after many painful years.

Your spirit will remain, eternally.
They did not understand that
you were quite extraordinary.
You broke all the barriers
before you, and discovered
many new and innovative
things to do. Your legacy
will live forever more.

It's you that we will
always adore.

Now, you rest in the arms
of the Lord. Your mind
and heart are on one accord.
Although we regret
that you are gone,
you must, gently,
sleep on.
You are loved.
You are missed.
Rest now,
Michael.

BIG MAMA

They Killed a Priest in 1965

They killed Father Jonathan in 1965. He was a priest who should have survived. This young man was in his prime. He lived in a despicable, shameful time. On a street in Alabama, he fell. Not a soul heard him yell. Alone, he was, on his walk to death. He died for neither fame, nor wealth. A young white man of the cloth was he, who came to town to help set us free. He was canonized for his bravery because he rejected acts of slavery. For him, they shed bitter tears. His memory will last for many years.

They killed this young priest with a gun. Thousands who read about it were stunned to hear of such a sacrilegious deed. As they mourned, their hearts did bleed. There were so many tears they did shed for this young priest who lay there, dead. They killed a priest in 1965,

but his spirit will never die.
May it never be said that
he died in vain for a precious
few. Only God knows
why he was sacrificed for
me, and for you.

Freedom cannot be denied
the children, the older folks and
people everywhere. We must
remember and forever care.
Know in our hearts that the
day he died, the whole world
prayed and they cried,
when they killed Father
Jonathan in 1965.

He is revered by the church he
loved. Those who mourned looked
to heaven above. For him, they
questioned the coming of a
day so dim. Then, a star
was discovered in the galaxy
for all who knew him to see.

They killed a young priest in 1965,
but he left us with a legacy and
gave his life with dignity as

he marched towards freedom for you and me. Part of our hearts also died when they killed Father Jonathan, in 1965.

Bells

Can you hear the bells ringing, and the little song bird singing sweetly in the morning breeze, amid the flowers and the trees? Close your eyes and hear them ringing, ever so gently. Stay a while and enjoy them. Savor the bells' melody. Listen. Can you hear them? I can hear them coming near, bringing joy, love, and cheer.

Red Bird

Yesterday, I saw a red bird sneak around my flower bed. He did not see me watching him steal the seed as he fled. He stole a bite, then with all his might, he flew towards

the sun, shining bright.
He lingered on a branch
all proud and boastful, after
his mischievous deed.
Back he came, repeatedly,
to steal more of the seed. I
spent hours watching him,
until the sun began to dim.
This little red bird sneaked
around on the tree limbs,
and on the ground.

Silk Roses

He gave me silk roses.
My heart was filled with woe.
Who gives a lady silk roses?
I really want to know.
Silk roses have no fragrance
like real ones, you see.
Why spend your time
sending them to me?

I like the sweet smell of fresh
roses. The aroma fills the air.
I like to wear fresh roses,
pinned in my hair.

> *"My love, the real ones fade,*
> *and you throw them away.*
> *Silk roses last forever,*
> *reminding you of*
> *me every day."*

Don't Y'all Know It's Spring?

[To my Northern friends, Bill and Cheyenne]

Fierce wind is blowing in your face.
Are the flowers budding? Not
a trace. In any case, don't
y'all know it's spring?

Snow is piled up to your knees.
Plows are flying down snow
covered streets, pushing
slush against red brick walls.
Don't y'all know it's spring?

Vehicles are slipping, sliding,
and colliding. Lights are flashing
all the time. Rescue squads are
stuck in long lines.
They'll never get there in time.
Don't y'all know it's spring?

Folks are wrapped up in sweaters,
coats, hoods, and blazers.
Wood's in the fireplace, blazing.
My back side's hot, and
my front side's cold!
Hey, y'all! It's spring!

Down South—barefoot children
are running in the front yard.
Folks are tooling around
in convertible cars. The heat is
beating down on our hair, while
snowflakes chill the air up there.
Don't y'all know it's spring?

Down South, old men are sitting
on white-washed porches,
sipping cold beer, telling lies,
remembering half truths, and
harboring twisted dreams of
past adventures, unrealized.
Don't y'all know it's spring?
Hey there, my friends!
Bill. Cheyenne.
It's spring!

The author (left) and other students from St. John's College (Santa Fe, New Mexico) are on a field trip to Chaco Canyon.

Woman

She totes the woes
of the world on her back—
An angelic sacrifice to
an undeserving land!
She holds her head high,
because she passed
the test of toil
and strife.
Her dark, wet eyes
never dry. There is a
constant stream of
loving care, as she
sees the morning as
a brighter day.

When the Dams Broke in New Orleans

When the dams broke in
New Orleans, my heart
was breaking, too.
I could not believe what
they let happen to you.
I saw the pain in your face.
How could they do this
to the human race?

There was water everywhere;
yet, they still left you there.
My sister, my brother.
When the dams broke in
New Orleans, my heart
was breaking, too…
…for you.

What Men Will Do

Men will swim an ocean,
fight the wildest beast,
climb the steepest mountain,
walk through fire, and spend
their last dime to be with
the woman they love.

Be Kind to Your Children

Be kind to your children.
During your golden years,
they might need to care for
you. They will remember
that you were, or were
not, kind to them.

~~~

Mama Bird and Baby Bird

Mama bird pushed baby bird
out of the nest. Baby bird
returned after a short rest.

Mama bird pushed baby
bird out of the nest again.
Baby bird returned quickly,
with a coy little grin.

Mama bird pushed baby bird
out of the nest a third time.
Baby bird did not return
to nest, or to dine.
Mama bird began to worry
about her little baby bird.
She searched and searched,
but no one had heard a word.

Then, mama bird found her
precious little baby bird.
Sweet noises from
the nest, she heard.
Mama bird perched on a
branch, gently, and watched
baby bird push her little ones
out of the nest, tenderly.

Barbed Wire and Basketball

They're behind barbed wire,
bouncing basketballs, or
standing against the wall.
That's how inmates pass
the day, on the rock in
San Francisco Bay.
Alcatraz is the name of the place
where bad guys come face to face
with the barbed wire that keeps them
in, so they can pay for their sins.

Basketball, their favorite thing,
is played at the far west wing.
They shoot hoops to forget
the things they now regret.
The tide rolls in from the bay,
but the inmates must stay

◄ BIG MAMA

on Alcatraz—the big rock,
where the cells are small
and doors are locked.

༄༄༄

I Couldn't Save You
(Slavery Era)

The overseer popped
his blood-caked whip,
and from your back
the flesh was ripped,
but I couldn't save you.
You glanced back at me
with teary eyes
bruised and blinded,
and I despised
the one who stripped you
of your dignity.

I waited in line to get my beating.
All the while you kept repeating:
*Save me from this horrible plight,
so that I can sleep throughout the
night.* I couldn't save you.
When you left the fields
five minutes too soon,
who would have thought
you would be doomed for

such an insignificant thing?
What misery it did bring.
I couldn't save you.

For centuries, I've wanted
you to forgive me, dear.
Your head is turned,
and you won't hear.
There was nothing I could
do, you see, to save
you, or to save me.

McDonald's is the World's Grocery Store

McDonald's is the world's
grocery store. I've seen what
people do. They buy a Big Mac
and to see them through,
they get ten of the straws, too.
Hands full of salt and pepper,
they sneak into their sacks.
Packets of ketchup and
a coffee cup will tide them
over until they come back.
McDonald's is the world's
grocery store. With all the paper
napkins there, ladies use them for
handy wipes, and for cleaning
milkshake from children's hair.

BIG MAMA

The straws are so very big,
meant for sipping colas and
such, but they're also good
for drinking soup when the
noon bell rings for lunch.
McDonald's is the world's
grocery store.
Don't say it's something you
don't do. We all go there to
get the sugar, and the salt
and pepper, too.
McDonald's is the world's
grocery store.
Enjoy the stuff
that's free!
Drive right up to
the parking lot,
and go shopping
for the week.

McDonald's and double decker bus in London (Piccadilly Circus).

Tribute to Women's Arms

Show your arms from
top to bottom. Thank the
Lord that you've got them.
Arms hold babies and
give great big hugs.
Why hide them? They
feel so snug.
Arms have reached across
the land, offering a helping
hand. So, reach right out
and extend your arms.
Express your beauty
and your charm.

Montmartre [Pigalle] Artists' Quarter - Paris, France.

You Complete Me

When I am weak, it's
his comfort I seek.
He completes me.

When I am sad,
he makes me glad.

When I feel down,
he erases my frown.

When times are tough,
his love is enough.

When I can't see the light,
he makes things bright.

In the cold of winter,
his touch is warm
and tender.

During a storm, he
protects me from harm.

When friends forsake me,
with a kiss he wakes me.

What would I do
without him?

When he is not near me,
my days are dim.

How could I live
without his love?

He's my dearest
friend, and my very
own beloved.
You see—he
completes me.

Happiness is Free

Happiness is free.
Knowing it is the key.
Why sit around and sigh,
or look for reasons to cry?
Life is too short to waste it.
Savor life. Taste it!

We Pause to Honor Great Women

We pause to honor great women.
We marvel at their warm hearts and
sentimental gestures. Their lives are
monumental beyond measure.
Their tasks --as steep as a mountain
that few will ever encounter.
Their commitments are a journey
for all the universe to see.

Behind their gentle nature we
find powerful, yet eloquent women
who stand before their audiences,
and justice they summon.
We pause to honor great women
who symbolize dignity and grace,
no matter what difficult
race they must face.

POETIC IMAGES

Sunlight in Your Eyes

Sometimes, on rainy days
when cold storms rage from
the dreary skies, I can still
see the sunlight shining
in your sad eyes. The glare
blinds me. I think of you,
back there on that slave ship
among the other lost souls.
As I gaze through my
mist-filled window, I wonder
how your centuries of freedom were
transformed into hopelessness.
I pray that you will recapture
the light that once shined
so brightly in your teary,
homesick eyes.

Harp

There is nothing more beautiful
than the melodic and seductive
music emanating from a harp.
God must have put his hand
on the harp's creation.
When the harpist is no
longer playing the instrument,
the melody lingers in the

air. Such effulgent beauty
captivates the spirit, and
takes one to a beautiful
and spiritual place.

How Beautiful I Am

When you look at me
what do you see?
The sparkle in my eyes
spans many centuries
of love and pain.

Let me show you
how beautiful I am.
I am not who you
saw yesterday, or
see today, or will
see tomorrow.
I am all these days.
I am the rising sun,
the sunset in the evening,
the shining night star
when the day is done,
and the clear moon.

Let me show you
how beautiful I am.

I am many faces.
I am the Ashanti
in deep Africa, and
independent Benin.
I am my sister in Algeria
with sand covering
my ebony feet.
I am Cleopatra,
claiming Egypt land
as her beloved.

My flesh is toasted
by the blistering
Moroccan sun.

The ocean releases my body
tossed overboard, spewing with
sanguine, scarlet redness.
They did not know me;
yet, they disgraced me.
This made me weep.
My wailing filled the
centuries with shame
for what they did to me.

I am the lost one,
and the found one.
I am the sad one,

and the happy one.
My soul is teeming
with love and chagrin.
My reflection shows
one who survived,
despite it all.

Once, hope was only
a word. I saw in it a
light that beckoned me.
I followed it.

I have lived through
incredible toils, unknown
to the rest of the world.
They said the sun did
not shine for me. I
beg to differ.

When I feel the heat of
the midday sun and the cool
mist of the evening dew, I
give praise to the One who
knows how incredibly
beautiful I am.

Don't Sleep in Flannel Pajamas
[To the Women of the World]

Don't sleep in flannel pajamas.
Silk ones will keep you warmer.
Flannel pajamas have
no personality.
Silk pajamas have so
much sensuality.

Ladies in silk get attention.
Flannel pajamas? No one will
even mention. Silk makes
you want to snuggle up,
and steal a few kisses from
your "butter cup."

Dump the flannel pajamas, or
just leave them in the drawer.
Reach for the pretty silk pajamas.
You'll enjoy them much more.

Sleep like a queen--
all wrapped up in your
cozy, silky dreams.

Children's Eyes

I see in the children's eyes
their fears, their hopes,
their aspirations, and things
that make them smile.
There is a quest for a life
that is fair and just.
I see in the children's eyes
the excitement that comes
from a loving home
with a father and a mother
in perfect harmony.
I see in the children's eyes
friendship and acceptance
of all of God's creatures—
big and small.
Sometimes, I see
in the children's eyes
confusion and questions:
Why am I here? Where
do I fit in this universe?
All that we were,
all that we are, and
all that we ever
will be is reflected
in the innocent
children's eyes.

Homeless Man

(Based on a true story)

The train carrying tourists stopped on its tracks. Next to the tracks was a homeless man sitting beneath a lovely bridge.

He wore tattered clothes, and used rusted pots, no doubt discarded by those more fortunate than he. His eyes were sad. His face showed no emotion.

"Perhaps, he was an architect and chose the lovely bridge as his shelter." someone said.

"See what the world has done to me." he seemed to say, as he sat there beneath the bridge. He stared at us. We stared back at him.
My heart sank.

BIG MAMA

Sitting there in my Klein
designs, sipping tea, I must
have seemed rather
bourgeois to this man
who made his home
beneath the rain
soaked, cold bridge.

For one quick moment, I
thought I saw a hint of
hopefulness in his eyes
when they met mine.

This soothed the
lump in my
burning throat.

As the train pulled
away, I raised my hand
and waved goodbye
to this sad, gentle,
homeless man whose
home was beneath
the cold, wet
bridge.
The train tour rolled on, but
I couldn't help thinking
of how fortunate I was

to be able to return
home to a safe and
secure place. From
that day forward,
I vowed to never
take any of my
blessings for
granted
again.

༄༅༅༄

Glass Pyramid in front of the Louvre Museum (Paris, France).

Big Mama has Something Else to Tell You

Papa

It doesn't matter whether
he is called father, papa,
pops, daddy, pere, padre, or
pa. If he is thoughtful, kind,
loving, and takes good
care of you, then
he is your DAD.

Mama

It doesn't matter whether
she is called mother, mama,
moms, mommy, mere, madre, or
ma. If she is thoughtful, kind,
loving and takes good care of
you, then she is your MOM.

RSVP

(Repondez, s'il vous plait)
[Respond, please]

(Adults Only Party)
This means:

* Do Not Bring *
Your children.

Your stepchildren.
Your grandchildren.
Your cousin's children.
Your cousin's grandchildren.
Your friend's children.
Your friend's grandchildren.
Jamal and Laquita's children.
No children!
Got it?

Idiot

If he acts like an idiot,
talks like an idiot, reasons
like an idiot, and treats
you like an idiot,
it's not likely that he
is anything else.

Procrastination

Procrastination means putting off, or delaying, projects that you know will improve your life. It is a fear that lives in every individual. This fear is conquerable, however.

BIG MAMA HAS SOMETHING ELSE TO TELL YOU

Stand up. Approach the task.
Look it square in the eye.

See yourself completing it.
Think of a reward that
you can bestow upon
yourself. When a person
procrastinates, the goals they
want to fulfill will remain,
forever, only a dream.

Electronic Madness

With the advent of cell phones,
blue tubes, fancy computers,
and other electronic devices, it
appears that some of the most
unpretentious persons are now
becoming gargantuan egoists.

Red Convertible, or Redhead?

Your husband wants to buy a
red convertible. So what?
Would you much rather
that he yearned for
a *Redhead?*

Buy Flowers Today

Why not buy flowers today?
Prepare a delicious meal.
Invite friends to your home.
A fresh bouquet of flowers
will brighten your dinner table.
Enjoy the seductive aroma
as you chat and dine.

Pity Party

When you feel down and out,
don't have a *Pity Party*. Have a
Freedom Party. Spend time with
friends. Read a good book. Take
a walk. Let the wind blow in your
face. Say to yourself, "I'm strong,
and I can handle anything."

Degradation

A person who degrades you
has to give up everything they
have to accomplish their goal.
You give up nothing. You are a
winner! What you keep is your
pride, self respect, and dignity
because you did not sink
to their level.

Americans and World Affairs

Many Americans don't seem to spend ample time studying world affairs. When something critical happens in the world, we ask, "How did that happen?"

Belief in God

Do you practice:
Faith
Charity
Daily Prayer
Compassion
Appreciation
Respect for Self
Respect for Others
Respect for Nature
Selflessness
Generosity
Humility

Men and Meals

There is nothing more satisfying to a woman than watching the man she loves enjoy a delicious meal that she prepared with her own hands.

Sit Down!

Don't you wish you could scream,
Sit Down! to people who stand up
at public gatherings, like concerts?
Everyone paid for the cost of tickets!

✂︎

Summertime in the 1960's
[Memphis, Tennessee]
Janice and Stephen sat on their front
porch rocking back and forth
in the green glider. They named
the model of each car as it passed
by on the gravel paved street.

They couldn't go to the public park,
because it was only open to white
children. They couldn't go to the
movies. Only white children could
sit downstairs where the floors and
seats were fresh and clean. They
resented having to sit in the
rancid, smelly balcony.

They couldn't go to the public
library where there were nice
wide tables, magazines, novels,
and other interesting books

in air conditioned rooms.
Only white people could
enter the library.

To break the boredom, Janice
and Stephen called together
all the children who lived on
their street. Then, they found
their tattered baseball mitts
and their old wooden bat, and
played ball in the street.

Afterwards, they sat in the
green glider on their front
porch, rocking back and
forth, and naming the
model of each car that
drove by on the gravel
paved street.

Ten Percent Better

As you begin each day,
why not make your life at
least ten percent better?
Improve your environment
by ten percent. Complete
tasks better by ten percent.
Live your life ten
percent better.

Preparing Meals

Statistics show that women prepare approximately 22,000 meals over a 20-year span of time. Don't forget to say, *"Thanks, mom."*

❧❧❧

Colored Water

Upon seeing the water fountain labeled "Colored" I rushed to partake of the cool colored water that glistened in the summer sun on that hot July day.
Lucky for me, the people standing nearby preferred the plain "White" water. Later, I pondered for hours their curious desires. I felt pity for those who, surely, must envy the soothing pleasure I enjoyed from drinking the colored water.

I pondered these things as only
a very young black child,
who does not understand
acts of segregation, ponders
such strange, curious,
and very bizarre
occurrences.

Child's Name

Why is it that as soon as a
child is born, the family
finds ways to shorten
the child's name?
Michael becomes Mike.
Susan becomes Sue.
Randolph is Randy.
Suddenly, Nicholas is called Nick.
Most children like their names.
Use them!

Thoughts

Thoughts are seeds
from which actions grow.
Lofty thoughts produce
unimaginable dreams and
incomparable success.

◄ BIG MAMA

Jekyll Island

Far down the beach on Jekyll Island,
I noticed a lighthouse in the distance.
Thinking it might be fun to get a closer
look, I began to walk along the
sandy seashore. As I walked towards
the lighthouse, I gathered some
of the beautiful, iridescent
shells that lay in my path.

A little man with long, skinny legs
walked ahead of me. He wore
a faded yellow print shirt
with flowers on the front
of it. His straggly, brown hair
was blowing in the wind.
This little man was having fun
disturbing the birds as
they played in the wet sand.
I thought that was a very mean
thing to do. As I continued
my long walk towards the
lighthouse, it seemed to
grow farther and farther
away from me. I couldn't
imagine what was happening.

Determined to see the lighthouse,
I raced pass the man in the
yellow shirt. He didn't notice
me because he was still busily
chasing the birds away
from the seashore.
I increased my pace, almost
to the point of collapsing.
And, although I was
panting from exhaustion,
I walked faster and faster.
I was overcome with the
determination to see
this lighthouse.

Imagine my disappointment,
when I soon realized that
what I thought was a beautiful
lighthouse was only a very
tall man, walking swiftly
ahead of me along the
sandy, wet seashore.

When All is Said and Done

When all is said and done,
you will find that you
can only depend on your
family. They will stand by you

in this world. They will take care of you while you live in this world. They will bury you when you leave this world. In the end, it's all about your family. Respect, love, and honor them.

Paper Plates

Wouldn't it be great if no one used paper plates? Fine china is hidden away, while the paper plates are used everyday. When company comes around, they enjoy the best. Respect your family as much as you respect the guests.

Housewife or Homemaker?

Are you so busy being a housekeeper that you have forgotten how to be a *homemaker*? Do you dust, polish, and idolize all your *stuff*? Concentrate on tending to the family. People are more important than things. Remember this!

Destiny and Fate

Destiny is the place at which we all arrive. It is predetermined. Fate denotes unfortunate incidents one encounters in pursuit of one's destiny.

Enablers

Beware of enablers. Enablers are people who encourage the weaknesses in others. This makes them feel needed. They are not helpful. They can worsen an already bad condition.

Earth and Water

I used to wonder why there was so much water on the earth. Then, it occurred to me that the oceans and the seas were meant for the inhabitants of the planet to travel upon them, to get to know one another and to live in peace.

The waters were never
meant to be used for
submarines and battleships
to carry torpedoes, and
deadly weapons of
mass destruction.

Travel the World

Visit Paris. Picnic on the lawn of the Eiffel Tower. Sit for a while at a café terrace. Enjoy a coffee. Watch the French stroll along the wide sidewalks on the Champs Elysees. Drive to the south of France. Swim in the crystal clear lakes. Pitch a tent on the beaches of the Mediterranean. Enjoy the deep blue sea.

Lovely Madrid. Everyone adores this beautiful city. Travel a short distance to Toledo. The awesome, brightly painted flower boxes lining the city will take your breath away.

BIG MAMA HAS SOMETHING ELSE TO TELL YOU

Return to enchanting Madrid.
Take time to watch a bullfight,
if you can endure it. The
brutality might be a bit
too much for you.

A Spanish matador slays the bull In Madrid, Spain.

Seductive Rome. Toss two coins
in the Trevi Fountain, hoping
to return to Italy some day. Say a
prayer for the unfortunate souls
who died in the clutches of
the wild beasts in
the Coliseum.

Brussels has its own unique
beauty. A land of lovely landscapes,
scenery, and marvelous plazas.
Sit and listen to the story of the
lost boy who was found playing, joyfully.

Geneva. Its streets are lined with
watch salesmen, competing for the
euro. Seductive fountains spew
beautiful, colorful water designs.
Snow-capped mountains
glisten in the distance.
Lovely Amsterdam. By day,
canals dominate the city. By
night, the waterways become
a romantic oasis. Take a
boat ride. Enjoy the view
of the lovely city.

Moscow. Mysterious and extraordinarily
beautiful. Its people stare in awe of
foreigners. They want to know who
you are. Walk through the Gum Department
Store. Find everything imaginable. Buy
a candy bar, or a car. This massive structure
will amaze you. Stop by Moscow's circus.
Enjoy the bears performing there.

BIG MAMA HAS SOMETHING ELSE TO TELL YOU

London. Fog is as thick as can be by night, and clear as a bell during the day. Shop Harrods. Visit Madame Tussaud's Wax Museum, the Parliament House, Westminster Abbey, and McDonald's! Fabulous discothèques light up the night.

A stopover in Iceland, land of green grass, quaint houses, and breathtakingly beautiful snow-capped mountains.

There is bittersweet Luxembourg, en route to Verdun. Thousands of American soldiers perished there, courageously—bayonets still visible through the sand and dirt, at this *Battle of the Bulge*. Cemeteries line the valleys. Soldiers who were not identified are honored by the eternal flame, honoring the Unknown Soldier. Travel the world. See how spectacular it is; yet, how somber it can be, as well.

Collectors

A person says, "I adore ceramics." That doesn't mean that the person should collect them from everywhere. Enjoy things for their historical value, uniqueness, and beauty.

Don't Care

Most men don't care what people say about them, or what others think of them. They just don't want anyone to get in the way of where they are going.

Tired and Lazy

Women don't like to say they are tired. They associate being tired with being lazy. Men are not hesitant about admitting they are tired. They will come right out and say, "I'm tired."

Artificial Turf

Two men lived in the same neighborhood. One envied his neighbor's beautiful, green lawn. He spent hundreds of dollars attempting to make his lawn more beautiful than his neighbor's, but to no avail.

Finally, giving up, he asked his neighbor how he was able to keep such a beautiful lawn. His neighbor replied, "I do nothing to my lawn. This is artificial turf."

Enjoy Your Treasures

Enjoy the things you value the most every day. Who should enjoy them more so than you? Don't save them for special occasions. Be good to yourself. Remember that you are the most important person in your life.

God Loves Us

God created the trees and the beautiful, fragrant flowers. We can thank him by doing some good deeds and honor Him by saying, "Thank you, God."

Crowd Gathering

Sometimes, when I see a crowd gathering for a special event, I yearn to see what all the fuss is about. The people seem so excited.

I hesitate, however, when the people assembled there do not look like me. I fear that this gathering might not be a safe place.

I often wonder if this fear will consume my life, forever.

Gardens

Visit a botanical garden. Walk
close to the flowers. Touch them.
Smell the fragrances. Enjoy
God's wondrous creation.

Who Am I?

I know the name they gave me.
I know the name I'm called.
I know where I was born.
Who doesn't, after all?
When I hear certain types of music,
especially drums in the big bands,
my heart picks up the rhythm
and I jump right up and dance.
In Africa, my kinsmen are free
to dance and sing to music
that is so dear to me. They live
in that faraway place. I long
to see them, face to face.

Mud

Sometimes, after the rain,
it's fun to go outside and wiggle
your toes in the mud. Do this--
just to be a little childlike. Try not
to be so serious all the time.

One Boot

When American soldiers march, there is often a very strict Sergeant who demands perfection. He takes pride in precision and unity. The Sergeant often yells, *"I want to see one boot!"* This is the way it should be with families. There should be respect and love; however, above all, there should be: *One boot!*

Home Cooking

After working all day, I'm in no mad rush to return home and cook pork chops, peel potatoes, bake hot corn bread, and make a big pitcher of sweet tea.

BIG MAMA HAS SOMETHING ELSE TO TELL YOU

Again, what did you say this was used for?

Weekend

I don't understand why people
who hardly know you will
often ask, "What did you
do this weekend?"
I respond, "Nothing much."
If I say, "Lots of things."
they want details.

Line of Fire

Guard you feelings. Don't
put them in the line of fire.
Hurt requires healing.
Your precious time
is too valuable
to waste.

Raising Children

When will society understand
that it is not the job of coaches,
teachers, and preachers to
raise its children? It is
the responsibility
of parents.

FICO SCORE

Beware of men who run
from woman to woman
trying to score.
What they might really
want to know is your
FICO score.

BIG MAMA HAS SOMETHING ELSE TO TELL YOU

Prejudice and Bias

When an opinion is formed about a person whom you never met, then it is likely that you are prejudice. Being bias is not the same as being prejudice. A person can be bias towards anything, such as food, colors, or even certain types of cars or clothing.

Cell Phones

A person who purchases a cellular phone for another person, and assumes that the phone will only be used to call them, has a lot to learn about people.

Pot of Gold

Don't tell your children, "There is a pot of gold at the end of a rainbow." Teach them how to attain their own pot of gold through perseverance and hard work. They will thank you.

Unscrupulous

Children can do such unscrupulous things. Do they remind you of someone you used to know?

Baking Soda and Vaseline

Can you remember when your teeth were whiter and your skin was softer, and you used only baking soda and vaseline?

Dropout

High school was all fun and games for you. Studying was something you would never do. Now, you want to stand in the long college lines. You've got to work extra hard since you are so far behind.

Getting Lost

Women always seem to know where they are going. Men often

get lost. Finally, men will say, "Well, I'll be dang! They have *re-routed* this street."

Shopping

Before purchasing an expensive item for a friend, why not think of some small thing to do for them? Write them a letter expressing what an awesome friend they are. Friendship can be shown in a variety of innovative ways.

Mean Spirited

Some people are just plain mean spirited. You can't change them. It's the way they are wired.

Bizarre

Some situations are so bizarre that all one can really say about them is, *"Oh, my goodness!"*

God's Garden

Select a small piece of the beautiful land with which you have been blessed. Plant a garden in honor of God and His goodness.
Call it: "God's Garden."

Parents and Children

Parents tell their children, "I want you to become a doctor, or a lawyer." Then, they buy them fire trucks and police cars. Why not purchase gavels and stethoscopes?

Impressing Others

Never do anything to impress others. Whatever you do should be done to enhance your own personal growth.

Men and Women

Women tell everything.
Men tell absolutely nothing!

Discounts and Promotions

When a customer decides to leave a company they are then inundated with all sorts of promotions and discounts. Where were these offers for the faithful customer before?

Flowers Blooming

Flowers blooming are God's way of saying, " I went shopping all winter and brought back something beautiful for you to enjoy during this spring season, because I love you."

Dream. Dream.

Dream as much as you wish to dream. Nothing happens, though, until you act.

Clinging Guys

Clinging guys can't bear to hear the words, *love or marriage*. They'll run faster than a roadrunner on a country road.

Men's Vocabulary

Men can often use a very limited vocabulary. They say: "Really?" "Oh, yes?" "I don't know." Some women hear those few words and talk for more than an hour.

Givers and Takers

The world is made up of givers and takers. Be very careful! Give discreetly. Accept with caution.

Dainty Diamond

Women say, "*I want a sweet, little dainty diamond ring.*" Forget about dainty! I want a diamond that makes a blind man see again.

BIG MAMA HAS SOMETHING ELSE TO TELL YOU

Disagreements

When I hear of nations
at war, I often
wonder if these
nations can remember
what the conflict
was about before
the war began.

The author finds the name of one of her high school classmates on the Vietnam Wall in Washington, D. C.

Enough Already

I truly believe everyone in the world would be much happier if the terms, "Whatever." "You are not listening." "Like." and "You know what I mean." were erased from the globe, *forever!*

❧❧❧

Men Don't Like Pumpkin Pie

Halloween was fast approaching. Megan wasn't going to let Halloween come and go without preparing a trick or treat feast for her husband.

There were several huge pumpkins lined up next to the pantry. Out of curiosity, I asked Megan what she intended to do with them. "I'm going to make some pumpkin pies."

I felt compelled to say what I was thinking. In the most unpretentious vernacular that I could conjure up, I said, "Girl, I thought you knew. Men don't like no pumpkin pie."

Crape Myrtles

Crape myrtles must be the most beautiful plants in the world. Anxious for my newly planted ones to bloom, I watered them, purchased expensive soil to speed them along, and watched over them like a mother hen. Despite my pampering, they still would not bloom. Finally, I gave up.

The next year, my garden blossomed with the beauty of the crape myrtles. I realized that, sometimes, you should leave things alone and let them grow naturally. The same is true in life.

Kindness

There are many people in the world who truly believe that being kind to *them* indicates that you surely must have lost your wits, or that you must be a weakling.
(That's sad.)

BIG MAMA

Letter to My Student

Did you say that your dad wasn't
there for you, and your mother
was the only parent at home?
Don't fret yourself! I saw how you
shot that basketball, from clear
across the room. I held my
breath when you ran those bases.
At the region Debate, you won
all the cases. With your great
personality, it's no wonder you
were voted, "Mr. Congeniality."
Your mother was so proud on
Saber Day. You stood so
straight and tall. We cried when
you went off to college, and said
your goodbyes to all. It was I who
sent you that $20.00 when you
graduated from Brown. I know
you'll be just fine in life, because
you seldom have a frown. Your
dad certainly missed out on a lot.
He'll never know what an awesome
guy he's got. Don't worry that you
never knew what having a father
was like. Keep reaching for the
stars, and always do what's right.

Your Teacher

England and Israel

England is America's "Big Mama."

Israel is America's "Sweetheart."

The World is a Playground.

Enjoy It!

This has been loads of fun.
Goodbye!

Acknowledgements

I am appreciative to my family for always believing in my ability to succeed. I extend gratitude to Dr. Carolyn Jackson, Dr. Shirley Jenkins, and Dolores (Dee) Crenchaw Singleton for their encouragement. My cousin, Magnolia (Maggie) Brison, is much more than a cousin. She is a friend who is relentlessly supportive. My high school classmate, George Puckett, encouraged me along this journey. I am thankful to my alma mater, Morris Brown College, whose tradition of excellence remains a cherished part of my life. I also thank Fredricka Douglas for enhancing my technological skills. I am grateful to Anna, my author representative, who insisted on excellence and accuracy throughout this process. I have the utmost respect for her. Lastly, I am appreciative to the talented cover designer for the very impressive book cover. This has been a true labor of love.

About the Photographs

Page 5. The author always enjoys checking out the Annual Atlanta Boat Show.
Page 13. Prom Promise (Sponsored by Nationwide Insurance). Students at Booker T. Washington High School sign a pledge to remain drug and alcohol free.
Page 44. Cathédral de Sacre Cœur, Paris, France. (Photo from the gallery of Sacre Cœur Cathedral.)
Page 46. Rodin's sculpture, The Thinker, in the gardens of the Rodin Museum in Paris, France.
Page 51. Illustration of how African women carried pottery on top of their heads.
Page 63. Photo of the author, taken after the funeral of Daisy Bates (1999), in front of Little Rock Central High School in Little Rock, Arkansas. (Daisy Bates, the author's aunt, was a mentor to The Little Rock Nine.)
Page 64. Sculptor, Auguste Rodin's *The Shadow* (L'Ombre). A gift from France to Atlanta, Georgia's High Museum after a tragic plane crash at Orly Airport. Atlanta artists perished there. (Photo from the Memorial High Museum).

Page 69.   Sculpture of a fallen American soldier at the Vietnam Memorial in Washington, D. C.
Page 80.   Three American soldiers. (Vietnam Memorial in Washington, D. C.)
Page 83.   The author and colleague, Louise Cox Byron, are extras (teachers) in the movie, Boy King.
Page 88.   The author takes a break at a café terrace on the Avenue Champs Elysees in Paris, France.
Page 89.   The author celebrates her promotion.
Page 102. The author and some of her colleagues from St. John's College (Santa Fe, New Mexico) are on an excursion to Chaco Canyon.
Page 109. McDonald's in London, England (Piccadilly Circus).
Page 110. Montmartre—Artists' section of Paris, France (Pigalle).
Page 121. Glass Pyramid in front of the Louvre Museum in Paris, France. (Photo, A Wolf/Explorer)
Page 137. A bullfight in Madrid, Spain.
Page 145. The author is about to prepare a meal.
Page 153. The author finds the name of a high school classmate on the Vietnam Wall in Washington, D. C.
Page 159. When she is not writing, the author enjoys driving around town in her red Mazda Miata MX-5 convertible.

Index of Titles

Absolutely Sure, 42
Acceptance, 20
Accumulating Stuff, 32
Admiring and Possessing, 8
Affirmative Action, 47
Alarm Clocks, 37
Americans and World Affairs, 127
Animals, 28
Apples, 15
Appreciation, 9
Architecture, 60
Arrogance, 42
Artificial Turf, 141
Attitude, 23
Baggage, 20
Baking Cookies, 12
Baking Soda and Vaseline, 148
Barbed Wire and Basketball, 105
Be Kind, 7
Be Kind to Your Children, 104
Be Quiet, 20
Be Yourself, 17

Beautiful Things, 47
Becoming A Parent, 17
Being Right, 40
Belief in God, 127
Bells, 98
Best Friend, 26
Best Friends, 30
Betrayal, 49
Beware, 53
Birds are on Fire , 66
Birds Share, 22
Bizarre, 149
Broken Mirrors, 40
Bully, 32
Burdens, 25
Buy Flowers Today, 126
Catching Up With Myself, 87
Cell Phones, 147
Challenges, 29
Character, 31
Child Abuse, 48
Child's Name, 131
Children are Different, 11
Children Grow Up, 54
Children's Eyes, 118
Clean My Garage, 84
Clinging Guys, 151
Cognizant , 37
Collectors, 140
Colored Water, 130
Common Sense, 37
Confident People, 28

INDEX OF TITLES

Cougars, 26
Courage, 29
Coward, 8
Crape Myrtles, 155
Creativity, 24
Crisis, 14
Criticism, 22
Crowd Gathering, 142
Curfews, 10
Dainty Diamond, 152
Deck of Cards, 28
Defining Yourself, 52
Degradation, 126
Destiny and Fate, 135
Disagreements, 153
Discounts and Promotions, 151
DNA and LOVE, 14
Documentation, 38
Don't Care, 140
Don't Sleep in Flannel Pajamas, 117
Don't Y'all Know It's Spring?, 100
Dream. Dream., 151
Dreams, 26
Dropout, 148
Earth and Water, 135
Electronic Madness, 125
Enablers, 135
England and Israel, 157
Enjoy Your Treasures, 141
Enough Already, 154
Excellence , 56
Family, 33

Feeling Down, 57
Feelings, 27
FICO SCORE, 146
Five Wars, 50
Fixing People, 38
Flowers Blooming, 151
Flowers, 55
Flutes, 32
Forgiveness, 25
Fortune Cookie, 28
Friends , 19
Friendship, 8
Friendships, 19
Gardens, 143
Genius, 36
Getting Lost , 148
Getting to Know a Man, 10
Gifted, 55
Givers and Takers, 152
God Created Woman, 56
God Loves Us, 142
God's Garden, 150
Good Man, 36
Good Morning, 33
Good Old Common Sense, 18
Great Books, 52
Grieving, 52
Guardian Angels, 56
Guilt, 58
HAITI, 54
Happiness is Free, 112
Happiness, 42

INDEX OF TITLES

Harp, 113
Harvard Tale, 72
Heartbreak, 15
Hero Has Died, 67
Home Cooking, 144
Homeless Man, 119
Honesty and Integrity, 31
House and Home, 41
Housewife or Homemaker? , 134
How Beautiful I Am, 114
Human Heart, 55
I Believe, 14
I Couldn't Save You , 106
I'm Sorry, 18
Icy Weather, 21
Idiot, 124
Impressing Others, 150
It is Your Life, 57
Jekyll Island, 132
Jokes, 9
Journey, 8
Jumping Off the Cliff, 30
Key to Success, 41
Keys, 40
Kindness, 155
Kissing Frogs, 33
Know It All, 17
L'Enfant, 78
Ladies and Gents, 16
Learning, 12
Lending Money, 36
Letter to My Student , 156

Letters and Emails, 58
Liars and Thieves, 41
Licking Your Wounds, 32
Life, 39
Line of Fire, 146
Listen and Learn, 27
Little Bit of something, 43
Little Voice, 22
Living Life, 60
Living Right, 43
Losing, 26
Love, 34
Loving, 12
Mama , 123
Mama Bird and Baby Bird, 104
Mama's Boy, 35
Mankind, 24
Marquette Park, 81
McDonald's is the World's Grocery Store, 107
Me • Myself • I, 48
Mean People, 38
Mean Spirited, 149
Meet the Date, 43
Men and Meals, 127
Men and Women, 150
Men Don't Like Pumpkin Pie, 154
Men's Vocabulary, 152
Mile in Someone's Shoes, 35
Milestones, 60
Mind Your Business, 43
Misbehaving, 60
Misfortunes, 10

INDEX OF TITLES ➤

Mud, 143
MUSIC, 50
Nasty Words, 22
Nations, 20
Ode to MIchael Jackson, 90
One Boot , 144
Open Mind, 19
Opinion, 35
Our Darkest Hour, 83
Owing, 24
Papa, 123
Paper Plates, 134
Parents and Children, 150
Past • Present • Future, 21
Pay Back, 54
Pay the Price, 27
People, 39
Pity Party, 126
Poet, 7
Possessing and Owning , 37
Pot of Gold, 147
Power, 34
Prayer, 48
Prejudice and Bias, 147
Preparing Meals, 130
Pressure, 24
Procrastination, 124
Projects, 49
Prophet, 47
Psychiatrist or Lawyer, 57
Purchasing a Car, 23
Rainbow, 29

Raising Children, 146
Reading, 57
Red Bird, 98
Red Convertible, or Redhead?, 125
Reflection, 39
Re-invent Yourself, 31
Remedy, 19
Respect, 30
Respect at Home, 31
Respect Children, 21
River of Love, 22
Rocking the Boat, 49
RSVP, 123
Sap, 15
Saying and Doing, 11
Schools, 13
Seeing, 32
Self Esteem and Ego, 16
She Ain't Mean, 61
Sheep, 34
Shopping, 149
Showing Off, 11
Silk Roses, 99
Sit Down!, 128
Snakes, 21
Solomon, 39
Some People are Crazy, 53
Something for Nothing, 30
Space to Grow, 44
Spending Time, 25
Squirrels, 52
Stars, 18

INDEX OF TITLES

Statue of Liberty, 70
Stick in the Mud, 16
Summertime in the 1960's, 128
Sunlight in Your Eyes, 113
Suntan, 9
Take Me Back to Mother Africa, 86
Take Over, 34
Talking Out Loud, 17
Talking to Children, 18
Tamed Horses, 36
Taste of Freedom, 9
Ten Percent Better, 129
They Killed a Priest in 1965, 96
Things You Don't Need to Teach, 23
Thoughts, 131
Time, 12
Time for a Friend, 50
Time for Yourself, 58
Tired and Lazy, 140
Traps, 41
Travel the World, 136
Tribute to Women's Arms, 109
True Friends, 55
Trump Card, 35
Truth, 15
Truthfulness, 7
Two Soldiers, 79
Understanding, 29
Unscrupulous, 148
Walking, 11
War, 70
Wars, 25

We Pause to Honor Great Women, 112
Weeds, 30
Weekend, 145
What are You Going to Do With Your Freedom?, 76
What Men Will Do, 103
When All is Said and Done, 133
When the Dams Broke in New Orleans, 103
Whisper, 38
Who Am I?, 143
Who are You?, 42
Why African American Women Wear Hats, 51
Wise Man, 33
Woman, 102
Women's Strength, 10
Words, 42
Work, 40
World's Problems, 27
Worthwhile, 40
Writing, 7
Writing and Knowing, 24
Years and Days, 15
You Complete Me, 110
Your Children, 9
Your Dreams, 14
Your Faults, 16
Your Heart, 48
Your Joy, 34
Your Life, 53
Your Name, 58

About the Author

Dr. Gwendolyn Jevita Cheatham graduated from Morris Brown College and began her teaching career in the Atlanta Public School System. After teaching for several years, she became the Instructional Coordinator of the Booker T. Washington High School Center for the Humanities Magnet Program. Pursuant to her interest in administration, she became an assistant principal.

She received her Masters degree in French from St. Louis University, and another Masters degree in Liberal Education from St. John's College in Santa Fe, New Mexico. She also graduated from Georgia State University with a Specialist degree in Education Administration and Supervision, and earned her Doctorate degree in the field of Educational Leadership at Walden University, in Minneapolis.

Harvard University selected Dr. Cheatham as one of the sixteen educators across the United States to receive a Grant for the study of Greek and Latin lyric. Her love of literature and zest for life inspired her to publish this extraordinary book.

LaVergne, TN USA
01 February 2011
214694LV00001B/47/P